# Usborne Little Wi
# Word Bo
# On the Farm

Illustrated by Marta Cabrol
Additional illustrations by Gabriele Antonini

Designed by Yasmin Faulkner
Edited by Felicity Brooks

# Farm animals

pig

cow

sheep

ram

goat

donkey

horse

bull

dog

pony

rabbit

cat

# The farmyard

farmer straw

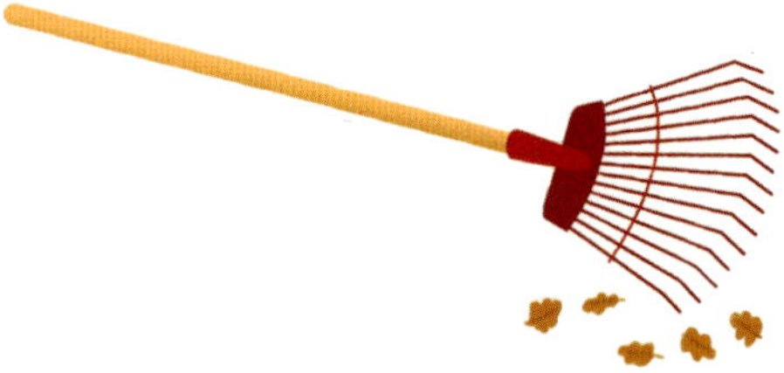

stable rake

broom bucket

farmhouse barn

kennel beehive

henhouse hutch

# Little animals

piglet calf

duckling kid

lamb chick

gosling foal

kitten puppy

rat mouse

# Farm machines

tractor trailer

livestock truck

power tiller

baler

milk tanker

crop sprayer

crop duster

pick-up truck

combine harvester

jeep

horsebox

# Birds on the farm

hen cockerel

turkey goose

duck barn owl

# Wild animals

squirrel deer

hedgehog fox

mole honeybee

# Food from the farm

bread

flour

eggs

milk

cheese

butter

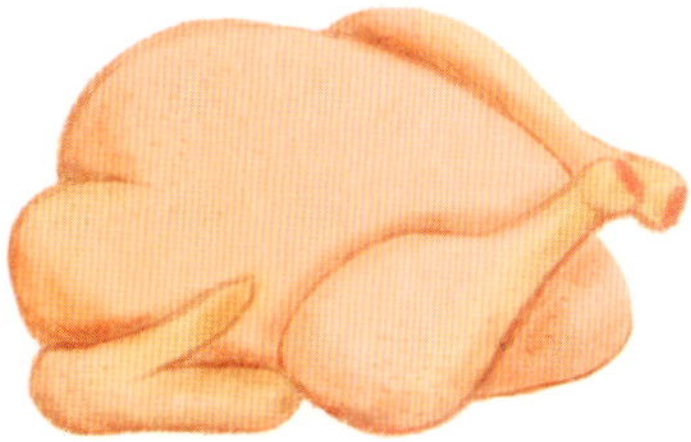

chicken beef

cream honey

apples berries

# In the farmhouse

teapot

sink

towel

scales

pan

oven

table

apron

rug

chair

plant

boots

# Vegetable patch

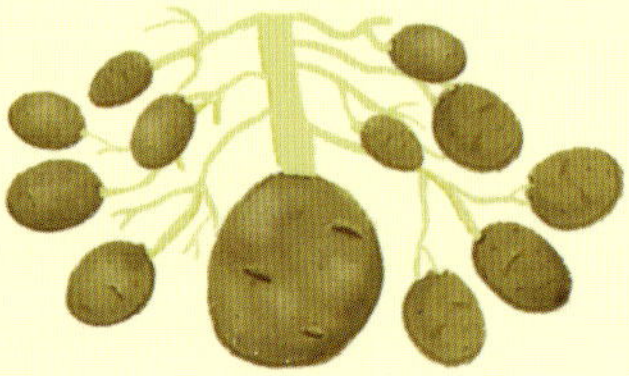

potatoes peas

maize tomatoes

cabbage carrot

onion pumpkin

courgette beans

turnip broccoli

# Around the farm

log scarecrow

trough hay bale

fork ladder

tree wall

gate fence

hill field

USBORNE

Usborne Little Wipe-Clean

# Word Book On the Farm

This fun book is a perfect way for young children to improve their language and writing skills by tracing over 130 farm words.

For advice about helping young children learn to read and write, and links to fun activities, go to www.usborne.com/quicklinks and enter the keywords "Early years activities".

£4.99
CAD$8.95

JFMAMJJASON /19
05429/1

Made with paper from a sustainable source.

www.usborne.com

ISBN 978-1-4749-6815-7

WARNING! Not suitable for children under 36 months because of small parts. Choking hazard.

ATTENTION! Ne convient pas aux enfants de moins de 36 mois en raison des petites pièces. Risque de suffocation par ingestion.

Ink from pen may not be washable.
L'encre du feutre ne s'efface pas toujours au lavage.

First published in 2020 by Usborne Publishing Ltd., Usborne House, 83–85 Saffron Hill, London EC1N 8RT, England. Printed in China.

tree wall

gate fence

hill field

# Farm noises

brrm

chug

woof

meow

baa

oink

moo

neigh

cluck

quack

cheep

ee-or

Usborne Little Wipe-Clean

# Word Book On the Farm

This fun book is a perfect way for young children to improve their language and writing skills by tracing over 130 farm words.

For advice about helping young children learn to read and write, and links to fun activities, go to **www.usborne.com/quicklinks** and enter the keywords "Early years activities".

**£4.99**
CAD$8.95

JFMAMJJASON /19
05429/1

Made with paper from a sustainable source.

www.usborne.com

ISBN 978-1-4749-6815-7
9 781474 968157 >

WARNING! Not suitable for children under 36 months because of small parts. Choking hazard.

ATTENTION! Ne convient pas aux enfants de moins de 36 mois en raison des petites pièces. Risque de suffocation par ingestion.

Ink from pen may not be washable.
L'encre du feutre ne s'efface pas toujours au lavage.

First published in 2020 by Usborne Publishing Ltd., Usborne House, 83–85 Saffron Hill, London EC1N 8RT, England. Printed in China.